Leading in The Dark seasons

PROACTIVE PRINCIPLES FOR SURVIVING WIDESCALE CRISIS

NICHOLAS SIBANDA

Published in South Africa by Nicholson Publishing™

www.nicholsonic.co.za

Nicholson™
Publishing

What leaders say

Leaders are visible more during a crisis. The author, Nicholas Sibanda makes a bold statement in his new book, *Leading in the Dark Seasons*. The practical and powerful message explodes throughout each page with encouragement for leaders to lead in tough times or get out of the way. If you are looking for a guide, handbook or reference when leadership is required for tough moments, this is your book. It takes you beyond inspiration to an attitude of taking charge when things fall through due to leadership vacuum.

Stanley Maphosa
President ABC Fellowship,
Founder Christian Business Directory and S3R Consulting
South Africa

The ever-changing face of global economics continues to give a new meaning to global commerce and business inter-connectedness. Global commerce is fast becoming an integral solution to global challenges like the COVID-19 pandemic or the challenge of feeding a growing global population with diminishing resources. Responsible leadership as a result, is not a "soft" management tool anymore, but a critical management function. Nicholas Sibanda's book is a must read! Responsible leadership and ethics are core lessons in this book. It is a very, very, very timely book! I thank God for giving him the vision to write this book. It blessed me.

Jonathan Mwaba
Chief Strategic Officer, Global Agribusiness Ventures Inc,
United States of America

I have known Niq for a long time and I have no doubt that the insights that are being shared in this book will add value to any minister that wants to serve the Kingdom mandate. It comes to me highly recommended.

Busani Mcingolwane
Founding Pastor, Kingdom Ways Ministries
South Africa

In *Leading in the Dark Seasons*, Pastor Niq has presented to us a very relevant and practical book that creatively, yet simply addresses the question of effective leadership in the face of the current crisis brought by the novel Coronavirus and of course any other situation. The book is unique in several ways: Firstly, it hits the iron while it is still very hot. Providing a manual for leading in crises while going through a crisis is very handy.

Duncan M. Chiyani (From the Foreword)
IFES Associate Regional Secretary for Southern Africa
Malawi

Crises have a habit of calling out leaders. They define them. They break them. They place a demand on them. In the Bible there is no better character than Joseph, who was called upon to lead Egypt during a major crisis. In this book Niq carefully shares with us the leadership principles that made and helped Joseph to lead better. It is easy to read, and the principles are practical. A must read for every leader.

Dr Phillip Tsvangira
Author of Where are the Fathers and Exceed,
Founder Institute of Christian Leadership
South Africa

Contents

Dedication

For leaders whose visionary leadership goes beyond the present disaster and give us hope for a better life after the coronavirus pandemic and to all leaders who will navigate future challenges and emerge victorious.

And…

To my review team who voluntarily invested hours of their time to read through the manuscript and gave me invaluable feedback as any reader would to make this a sound readable book.

My gratitude is sincere.

Foreword

I first met Nicholas Sibanda in 2007 in Ontario, Canada while attending an International Fellowship of Evangelical Students (IFES) World Assembly. Both Niq and I were on staff with our IFES National Movements in Zimbabwe and Malawi respectively. We spent a little bit more time together after the World Assembly as we were both hosted by a mutual friend for a couple more days in Toronto. What was clear from my initial meeting for me was his passion for Ministry in the areas of Disciple-making, Mentorship, Social Justice and Strategic Development. We have met several times after that. Most recently, at another IFES World Assembly in July of 2019 in South Africa and again in September of 2019 in Zimbabwe, where we were both speakers at a National Students' Conference.

All these meetings gave us opportunities to engage in meaningful discussions on Spiritual growth, Social Justice and Strategic Development. We have talked about leadership in various spheres of life; and I must confess that the conversations have always been beneficial in my personal and Ministry life. Recently, I became one of the recipients of his online blog on Entrepreneurship, which I find very relevant for my personal capacity building.

In *Leading in the Dark Seasons*, Pastor Niq has presented to us a very relevant and practical book that creatively, yet simply addresses the question of effective leadership in the face of the current crisis brought by the novel Coronavirus and of course any other situation. The book is unique in several ways:

Firstly, it hits the iron while it is still very hot. Providing a manual for leading in crises while going through a crisis is very handy. As I went through it, it presented an unprecedented relevance to my country's COVID-19 situation that I plan to hand it to the authorities to reflect on the blueprint for our response. It also challenged me as an individual on how to lead my family beyond COVID-19 and building cushions for the future. Secondly, it addresses multiple aspects with such simplicity. It deals with spirituality and character, social justice as well as strategic thinking, planning and execution without complicating the discourse.

Using everyday language, Pastor Niq has managed to draw valuable lessons for leaders and followers in Dark Seasons and beyond. Thirdly, his use of a well-known Bible story yet bringing out lessons from aspects we usually never think about, adds to the book's uniqueness. I have read the story of Joseph many times like many of us, but I have never paid much attention to the rescue plan and how people responded to it. Pastor Niq brings out the challenge of most citizens' over dependency on the State especially in times of crises. The concept of generosity coming from abundance at an individual level is very sobering and Biblical too.

The book brings hope for the future and offers suggestions that could materialize that hope. He discusses the role of what he calls the "Spirit of Entrepreneurship" that was in Joseph and draws parallels on how that could be so relevant in our time. He says leaders are to identify opportunities, set targets to work towards, mobilize resources at their disposal, plan for long term and understand their working environment.

He further challenges leaders to be decisive during crises, to build cordial relationship with people so that they buy into the leaders' decisions to work hard towards achieving the targets. He challenges leaders to take up the leading challenge regardless of their personal hurts, which they must work on while leading, while making sure that those hurts are not clouding their judgment. Leaders are to use their power for the greater good.

Pastor Niq's conclusion to the book is a call for leaders to *mentor* people with potential, to lead with *responsibility* and make sure they own up their mess, to lead with *maturity* not taking personal grudges into leadership, exercise *authority* with caution, provide *resources* to people they delegate, to be *accountable* when entrusted with resources in times like these and above all to *serve the people* because leadership is given on trust that you will serve the people.

Leading in the Dark Seasons is a good read for anyone who is serious about leadership and indeed to any individual who would love to deal with life crises and grow. I recommend this book heartily.

Duncan M. Chiyani
IFES Associate Regional Secretary for Southern Africa

Preface

My son Jonathan is eight years old. He wrote the following poem after weeks of listening to warnings, his school days cut short and two weeks of lockdown and countless reprimands for slipping out of the house to play with his buddies. It was composed as any 8-year-old can compose, but reflects the mood of the times:

About Corona

Corona stop killing people
Corona closed schools
People stay at home
They are afraid of you
You are like a lion in a jungle
Waiting to eat a baby zebra
You killed innocent people
You are bad corona.
Please corona stop.
Please corona. Please corona.
You killed people.
What is next? Take over the world?
But we have sanitizer and soap.
And one thing please, please find another place to go
You must leave us alone.
When you go, we will be happy.
Keep hands clean. Everyone; stay safe stay alive.
Keeping hands clean is important.
Keeping hands clean is good.
- ***Written by Jonathan Sibanda***

(We are publishing this poem as an illustrated children's book and the part of the proceeds will be donated to efforts to prevent COVID-19 in Jonathan's school.)

Introduction

The role of leadership has never been easy. This book is written as a reflection on some leadership principles that shine through one of history's episodes of disaster. The name of Joseph the son of Israel is tucked away in the narrative of his father in the first book of the Bible and yet yields much value for leaders of all generations on how to deal with times of crisis and widespread disaster.

This story is revisited in the context of the early days of the novel coronavirus that took the world by surprise at the start of 2020. Leaders at all levels rose up to the challenge. Others did well and others not so well. But that is what crisis does, it tests the quality of leadership. One of the most important leadership lessons from Joseph's story is to lead with a long-term focus. To think about the future. The success of our leadership is often measured in the accomplishments in our lifetime. Joseph shows us that it matters how things pan out when disaster strikes.

The coronavirus pandemic seems to have altered the history of the world in just three months. The future will depend more on the quality of leadership decisions than resources, scientific advancement and other factors that we normally utilise to measure capacity to handle challenges of a global magnitude.

Nicholas Sibanda
Johannesburg, April 2020

Chapter 1

The Outbreak

The end of the year 2019 saw the outbreak of the coronavirus disease, (COVID-19) apparently in Wuhan City, China. The disease is caused by the viral infection by the novel corona virus, a part of the virus family that includes the SARS and MERV viruses that have broken out in Asia in recent years. The virus is spread from one person to another via the infected individual's respiratory droplets or contact with surfaces that harbour the virus from the infected individual such as metal, plastic etc. Because the virus is still being investigated, much is yet unknown and as such, information about it keeps changing with new study results being made available.

The virus outbreak history is still shrouded in mystery. The commonly accepted theory almost feels like it came from the script of the 2011 movie *Contagion*! The virus is suspected to have moved from some fruit-bat to humans in Wuhan's wet market. (A wet market is a market where live animals or freshly slaughtered animal food products are sold directly to the consumer. These would include bats, pangolins, chickens, pork and a host of wildlife.) These markets exist in several parts of the world and are generally notorious for the local outbreak of infectious diseases from time to time.

Coronavirus infection Timeline

The virus behaviour and statistics reflect the current trends at the specified time and continues to change significantly. (Refer to updated statistics). However, the patient zero to 2milllion reported infections came within four months. The second million was infected within 14 days!

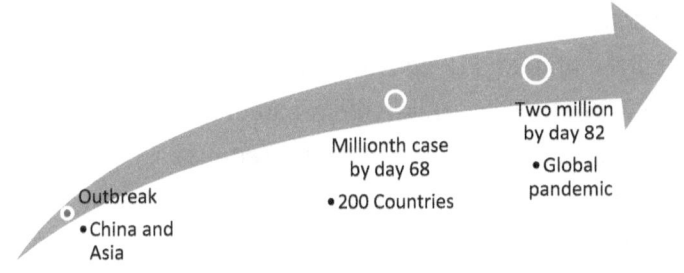

Millionth case
by day 68
• 200 Countries

Two million
by day 82
• Global
pandemic

Outbreak
• China and
Asia

-    *Stats source: WHO (April 13)*

Conspiracy theories

Like many such unfortunate global afflictions, the coronavirus spawned a host of conspiracy theories when it started making landfall beyond the Chinese shores. *The Bulletin of the Atomic Sciences* published an article on March 13 titled; *Why do politicians keep breathing life into the false conspiracy theory that coronavirus is a biological weapon?* The article stated that; "For political opportunists and conspiracy theorists, the rising number of COVID-19 infections, the growing ranks of the dead, and the mass disruptions to the daily rhythms of life have created fertile conspiratorial ground."

Biological weapon

The US Senator Tom Cotton was the chief proponent alleging that the virus was a bioweapon of Chinese origin. This theory got support from the former Iranian president Mahmoud Ahmadinejad, who pointed the finger at the USA. The Chinese Foreign ministry spokesman Lijian Zhao also accused the USA. In an article published on March 12, *Express*, a UK tabloid, claimed that there was evidence that coronavirus was a bioweapon leaked from the Chinese research labs near Wuhan City. This one will likely take a long time to settle.

Population control

This is the age-old theory of someone trying to cull the global population so that they can utilise the resources. The Chinese were the alleged culprits in one version. Because China has limited resources and must depend on the rest of the world, they then created a virus to kill everyone and colonise the world. The other version was fingering the Pirbright Institute in England as working with former Microsoft CEO, Bill Gates.

The 5G radiation

The introduction of 5th generation, high speed internet in several developed nations is blamed for the emission of an excessive radiation signal that causes symptoms that are like corona virus. This theory claims that the virus is a hoax for the deadly radiation. The claim is that Wuhan City has the highest concentration of 5G terminals in the world (10 000, it is alleged). The virus, at least in its early days, seemed to grow the fastest in the technologically advanced countries where

5G is already in use including several cruise ships which were allegedly fitted with the technology.

The Illuminati

As in most things that have a trace of control of world finance and markets, the secret society called the Illuminati was fingered as having used this to manipulate global markets to gain control of the finances of the world. The illuminati are generally said to be composed of the world's richest individuals and a host of celebrities with an insatiable desire for world domination, eagerly waiting to pounce on any opportunity to introduce their New World Order.

Apocalypse

Almost every destructive plague, has always triggered the end-of-the-world panic buttons. The COVID-19 outbreak was no exception. Prophets stepped forward and claimed to have foretold this. Churches filled up as the faithful and prodigals alike sought to get right with their Maker. Even the ancient prophecies of Nostradamus in 1555 started doing the rounds.

There have also surfaced claims that racist Europeans want to test the vaccines on Africans and allegations of contaminated masks are being shipped from China to poor countries to spread the infections. These falsehoods and half-truths as well as manipulation of facts and figures are standard for any crisis of such global proportions.

All these will continue to abound so long as there is no cure found and people feel fearful. Social media helps these claims spread far and wide before they are tested. Sadly, no one comes back to own-up after the myth is debunked! The attempt to control these often infringe on the freedom of speech and expression creating a Catch-22 situation for regulators. The information mashup will continue as it is often hard to distinguish truth from fiction immediately.

Impact on life

Conspiracy theories aside, the impact of the virus on the world has been devastating to say the least. Within three months, it had become a global pandemic leaving thousands dead in its wake. Nations responded in unprecedented fashion, enforcing extended lockdowns, shutting their boarders and quarantining any cases detected through extensive screening and testing initiatives. Life in a country with nearly 60% of the economy in the informal sector, entrepreneurship still at infancy and millions depending on the state for handouts is a bleak reality.

However, there are two critical factors that were game-changing 1) decisive leadership and 2) corporate citizenship. These seem to have been key in helping most countries stem the tide of the virus in its initial stages. Governments that committed themselves to lockdown, poured in funds into educating the masses on washing hands, maintaining social distance and identify and quarantine methods managed to effectively slow down the spread by "flattening the curve." But despite all these initiatives, the loss of production, close of businesses, sudden disruption of value chains, forced confinement and extended relief expenditure took its toll on the household and national resources. The downstream effects will likely be felt in the future on the long term.

Death and recovery by numbers

The rate of infection globally, has continued to climb exponentially. In most cases faster than can be identified and traced because there is no vaccine or adequate resources like facemasks, ventilators or even hospital beds to manage the spread of the virus. Although the recovery rate among the infected was noteworthy. The global infection rate was climbing quickly.:

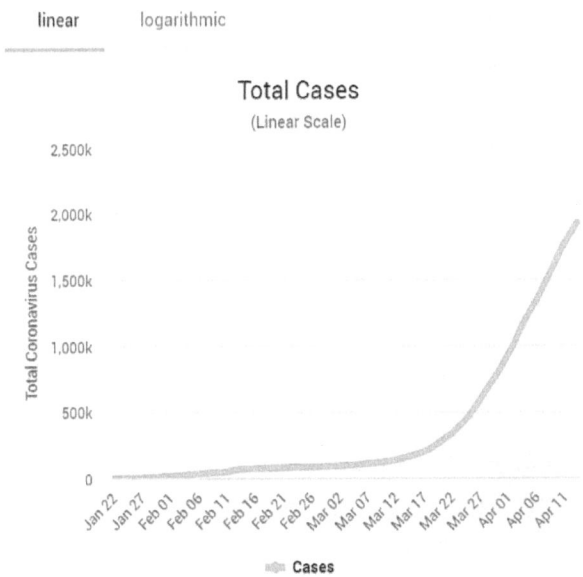

Source: Worldometer (13 April 2020)

The death figures were equally grim with speculation that they could spike sooner or later.

12

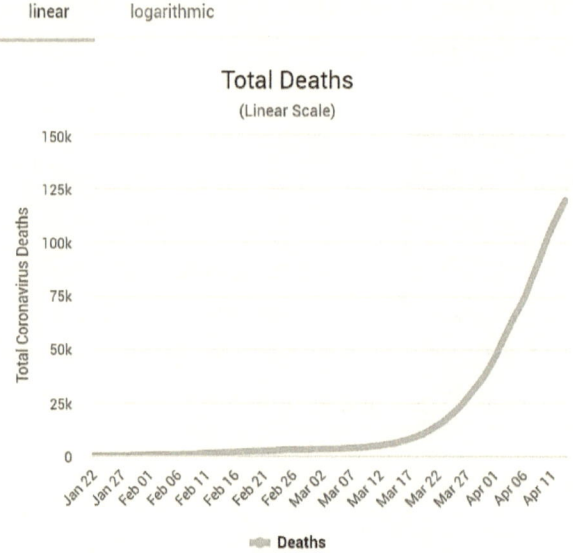

Total Deaths
(Linear Scale)

Source: Worldometer (13 April 2020)

Responses

The outbreak of the COVID-19 virus and its swift escalation into a pandemic had drastic implications for leadership at all levels of society. The new routines for survival were washing hands with soap or a sanitizer and maintaining social distance. This was the hardest implication of these new rules that had to be enforced strictly. Loved ones were buried or cremated by undertakers on their own, sometimes in mass graves. Sweeping lockdown rules disrupted life's social aspects. No school, no work, no travel. Coupled with the uncertainty of containment, these took their toll on the psyche of all nations.

The initial global response was that of fear and panic. Most countries simply followed what their peers did but had no real

13

plan or capacity for the management of the pandemic. There are several factors about the virus that inspired the world to respond in the way that it has done.

- This is a new virus
- The rapid global spread
- Strain on even the best healthcare systems
- Vaccine prospects in 18-24 months
- Rising death toll

Spiritual

The disease's clampdown on humanity and its anticipated long-term impact has sent the world to seek Divine intervention. Prayers have been going on despite the scientific methods such as washing of hands with soap, maintaining social distance and staying home. Unlike any other natural challenge, the coronavirus has revived faith like no other in recent human history. Once it became apparent that science was presently limited to deal with the pandemic, people across the world and religions took to prayer earnestly.

The South African president requested the nation to join in a season of prayer at the onset of the initial 21-day lockdown. The Kenyan president declared a day of prayer in the face of the threat of the coronavirus stating that the nation had turned to God for his blessings in good times and that this was the right time to turn to God for help.

At this time protesters against 'imposing prayer on people' seem to be looking the other way as health officials in the USA and UK are seen praying for each other and for patients.

These are tough times that call for unprecedented measures. At the time of publication, prayer chains and calls were still a common occurrence on many public media platforms.

Economy

The principal concern for many a nation is always the economy. The global economy of the 21st century is so interconnected that an outbreak like this has devastating consequences for every nation on earth. Production is down. Travel is banned. The informal sector that forms the vast end-user consumer market is at a standstill. Countries are drawing on their reserves to sustain their people alive. Most of the initial responses were designed to shield the economy, but when the virus continues to take the best and more from among us, one is left wondering what will be left of the economies of the world.

Technology

It is true that our scientists and doctors and researchers are working round the clock trying to find the vaccine. We are a technologically sophisticated people. We are almost sure to find the vaccine. But for now, we all acknowledge that the crisis is beyond our sophistication. It is important that we recognise this because our reliance on science has driven us to heights of arrogance! Technology thrives with humility, we are learning that now, it seems.

Politics

The battle against the spread of the virus has been won or lost mainly on political leadership. Regular briefings, difficult decisions and keeping the pulse on every corner of the country while keeping an eye on the developments across the world can wear any politician out. The activation of emergency laws, enforced by security forces, as well as other laws that enable health departments access to emergency government funds for the vulnerable were all, thanks to proactive government leadership. In cases of ineffective leadership, governments chose propaganda, misinformation and secrecy and repression to control the masses. The consequences for their people are going to be catastrophic in the long term.

Political leaders are the rallying point during crisis of this magnitude. The intense juggling was best exemplified by Cyril Ramaphosa, the South African President who on announcing the national lockdown had a press briefing in his suit and charged the armed forces to enforce the lockdown rules in his army uniform just a few hours later!

The Botswana President endured a two-week quarantine after a suspected exposure while on an official visit to neighbouring Namibia. As he was getting his country ready for its lockdown, all the country's parliamentarians were required self-isolate due to exposure during a COVID-19 screening for MPs.

In the UK, the Prime Minister was hospitalised and at a stage, in ICU after contracting the virus. His hospitalization was not shrouded in secrecy and he was treated at a London hospital where fellow Britons were also hospitalized. Upon recovery, he thanked the hospital staff and affirmed the value of the National Health System. There have been many opportunities for great leadership to shine in these times!

Humanitarian

Because life does not stop during a crisis, effort from relief organisations, state welfare and generous citizens have been invested through solidarity funds set up for alleviating the negative impact of the virus especially on the vulnerable and managed through non-governmental organisations (NGOs) and government agencies. This saw the provision of food parcels, temporary shelter for the homeless, relief funding for small businesses and other professionals that lost income through the lockdown periods or due to the disruption of their markets. Reassuring people, caring for them and comforting the bereaved fell upon both the state and the citizen.

Medical

The medical fraternity bore the burden both physically in extended hours and constant emergency status as well as emotionally. It is stressful to lose a patient, we are told, but to lose thousands daily can break even the toughest medical practitioner. Some took unprecedented risk working in the frontlines, sometimes without adequate personal protective equipment. There were instances of collaboration between the private and public sectors of the health industry and between countries in helping manage the spread of the disease. This is leadership at work.

Fear of opportunists

A global crisis of this magnitude attracts criminal elements, and it is not surprising that some of the fears that we share are not unfounded. In certain countries the state has authorised itself to access private personal information to enable health workers to trace potential contacts in the case of those who test positive to the virus. Many worried about the security of their information in the hands of government especially in the era of cyber-crime and potential repressive state authority.

In South Africa, reports emerged early into the lockdown, of criminals masquerading as health officials or soldiers robbing, raping and killing victims. There were many alarmists and peddlers of falsehood too, making business out of fear and misinformation. Some of the conspiracy theories led to citizens spurning screening and testing initiatives by government after the 'contaminated Chinese test kits' stories surfaced. It is an undesirable but not a far-fetched idea that the bickering spats between global powers could even spark a war.

Recovery rate

One of the most welcome factors about COVID-19 must be the recovery rate in its early months. It is those people who responded to prayer or to the treatment of the symptoms of the disease and recovered. It is those whose immune systems battled the infection and won in self-isolation or quarantine and even those who were infected but never developed the symptoms.

That gives us hope in the face of the thousands that were buried in mass graves daily in some parts of the world. It gives us hope that a vaccine is possible. That humanity will survive this great scourge. When the number of infections was at 1991275 the closed cases showed that 79% had recovered and 21% died. *Source: Worldometer (13 April 2020)*

Reason for hope

The global economy is expected to go into recession and yet the end of the scourge is not in sight. Gloom and doom are being forecast for both the short and long term. The media of our day is super pessimistic and thrives on woe and doom. We need to look back at how nations recover after these types of catastrophes. Whatever the crisis, there is a formula already, so we do not need to reinvent the wheel.

How did we emerge from the 2008 financial crisis? How did Germany recover after the Nazi disaster? How did Japan recover after the war and the nuclear bomb in Hiroshima? How did America recover after the great recession in the 1930s? How did Rwanda recover after the 1994 genocide to be a leading nation in Africa? Yes, there post-Soviet eastern European nations, and China, which not so long ago was in grinding poverty? The list is long. The question is not "if", but "when". As in the cases above, everything depends on those who lead in the crisis.

Chapter 2

Leading in dark times

A few years ago, I read a critique of Joseph's philosophy as Prime Minister in Egypt by Guy Brandon in a Christian journal. To be honest, it was before I learnt to critique my Biblical heroes and appreciate their shortcomings despite the great works they wrought for their God. Joseph was my squeaky-clean hero who saved the day - period. He not only saved the Egyptians, but the entire ancient civilisation and their political system and paved a way for the hosting of God's people where they transformed from a single family into a nation.

However, Brandon argues that while his 20% tax regime may have been justifiable, his political ideology wasn't sound e.g. centralised approach to economic management, taking money out of circulation and the subsequent enslavement of the Egyptians would lead to disastrous future consequences for the Israelites in Egypt. Leaders in COVID-19 times are faced with similar decisions that may lead to massive disruption of people's way of life and economic ruin.

Who is this Joseph?

Joseph was born into a typical dysfunctional family, which had problems that looked more like a modern TV soapie family. There was bitter polygamous rivalry. His father who was once a fugitive from a family feud, got exploited by his uncle who later became his father-in-law. The kids in this family bore names that were meant to convey a threat or taunt to the rival wife. In fact, Joseph's name means - *a son shall be added*. And his brother Benjamin came at the cost of their mother's life (she died of childbirth complications). As if that was not enough pain for the young lad, his brothers hated his guts because his old man showed blatant favouritism towards him.

Coming to Egypt

One day they hatched out a plan to get rid of him and sold him off as a slave to some traders going to Egypt. He exchanged hands until he landed in the household of one of Pharaoh's senior officials. Life seemed to get better until he was framed for attempted rape by his boss' wife who felt scorned by his refusing her advances towards him. Prison time was his final stop before he began his ascent. While serving time, he began to interpret dreams and did so for two of Pharaoh's household officials predicting the acquittal of one and hanging of the other. But the guy who was saved forgot him for two years!

Then Pharaoh had a series of strange dreams that troubled him a great deal. As he sought the answer, the official whose dream Joseph interpreted two years prior, remembered him. Joseph was sought out and brought before Pharaoh. This is where we begin to examine his story as a government official.

It is this background that he has as he assumes the highest administrative position in the land. Except, there is a little caveat – he had the Spirit of God in him. That was at least Pharaoh's rationale in appointing him after he successfully interpreted his dreams.

The story is detailed in Genesis 41:17-43:

The Dream and Interpretation

Then Pharaoh said to Joseph, "In my dream I was standing on the bank of the Nile, 18 when out of the river there came up seven cows, fat and sleek, and they grazed among the reeds. 19 After them, seven other cows came up — scrawny and very ugly and lean. I had never seen such ugly cows in all the land of Egypt. 20 The lean, ugly cows ate up the seven fat cows that came up first. 21 But even after they ate them, no one could tell that they had done so; they looked just as ugly as before. Then I woke up. 22 "In my dreams I also saw seven heads of grain, full and good, growing on a single stalk. 23 After them, seven other heads sprouted — withered and thin and scorched by the east wind. 24 The thin heads of grain swallowed up the seven good heads. I told this to the magicians, but none could explain it to me." 25 Then Joseph said to Pharaoh, "The dreams of Pharaoh are one and the same. God has revealed to Pharaoh what he is about to do. 26 The seven good cows are seven years, and the seven good heads of grain are seven years; it is one and the same dream. 27 The seven lean, ugly cows that came up afterward are seven years, and so are the seven worthless heads of grain scorched by the east wind: They are seven years of famine. 28 "It is just as I said to Pharaoh: God has shown Pharaoh what he is about to do. 29 Seven years of great abundance are coming throughout the land of Egypt, 30 but seven years of famine will follow them. Then all the abundance in Egypt will be forgotten, and the famine will ravage the land. 31 The abundance in the land will not be remembered, because the famine that follows it will be so severe. 32 The reason the dream was given to Pharaoh in two forms is that the matter has been firmly decided by God, and God will do it soon.

The Proposed Solution
33 "And now let Pharaoh look for a discerning and wise man and put him in charge of the land of Egypt. 34 Let Pharaoh appoint commissioners over the land to take a fifth of the harvest of Egypt during the seven years of abundance. 35 They should collect all the food of these good years that are coming and store up the grain under the authority of Pharaoh, to be kept in the cities for food. 36 This food should be held in reserve for the country, to be used during the seven years of famine that will come upon Egypt, so that the country may not be ruined by the famine."

The Response
37 The plan seemed good to Pharaoh and to all his officials. 38 So Pharaoh asked them, "Can we find anyone like this man, one in whom is the spirit of God?" 39 Then Pharaoh said to Joseph, "Since God has made all this known to you, there is no one so discerning and wise as you. 40 You shall be in charge of my palace, and all my people are to submit to your orders. Only with respect to the throne will I be greater than you."

The Appointment
*41 So Pharaoh said to Joseph, "I hereby put you in charge of the whole land of Egypt." 42 Then Pharaoh took his signet ring from his finger and put it on Joseph's finger. He dressed him in robes of fine linen and put a gold chain around his neck. 43 He had him ride in a chariot as his second-in-command, and men shouted before him, "Make way!" Thus he put him in charge of the whole land of Egypt.
– NIV*

Looking forward

Seven years of positive bank balances and abundance were coming. Then seven years of severe famine that will completely overshadow the years of abundance were coming. The proposal that Joseph made in v33-36 was a success formula for the next 14 years! This was not a state secret or mere government policy. It was a success formula that could work for any private Egyptian citizen who put it into practice.

The fascinating thing in this story is the response of the Egyptians. Brandon reflects on this by stating that: *"[Joseph] could have tried to convince the people to save grain for themselves, though he probably would have been unsuccessful. In any case, the seven years of plenty must have seemed like an economic boom, doubtless accompanied by the same irrational optimism that accompanies every bubble: the good times will never end!"*

Herein lies the challenge of all successful generations. They view success as a goal to be achieved rather than a means to an end. We often measure people's success by how much one has in the bank. We call it their net worth. There is no poorer way to view wealth. In our narrative, the interpretation of the dream was clear in v29-31:

> *29"Seven years of great abundance are coming throughout the land of Egypt, 30 but seven years of famine will follow them. Then all the abundance in Egypt will be forgotten, and the famine will ravage the land. 31 The abundance in the land will not be remembered, because the famine that follows it will be so severe." NIV*

This is where the Egyptians missed the point as do most of us who form what we referred to as poor nations! The policies and formulas for the success of the richer nations are an open secret, but we never take them seriously. Yes, politics tells us that they steal from us, but the truth be told, they have developed their capacity to leverage from a position of strength.

> *The rich rule over the poor, and the borrower is servant to the lender. - (Prov 22:7) NIV*

Most of us have never ventured to develop our own resources. We take the loans willingly for consumption. We appoint corrupt officials. Our best people run away to these 'evil' nations and provide them their best intellectual abilities and we suffer perennial brain-drain and lack of creativity.

We have examples of nations that have changed their trajectory like Japan, Korea and China who were considered poor nations not so long ago, but aggressively worked their way out of dependency on the handouts from the rich nations. Most of the poor nations of the world still export raw materials and their ideas to the rich ones only to pay many times more for the finished products they import back! The way to success is clearly demonstrated, yet we still wallow in poverty!

Joseph produced a fool proof plan to cope with the impending crisis, but most people put their hope on the state. They squandered 80% of their produce in the years of abundance. Note that these were not regular good years. They were years of abundant plenty, above the regular harvest.

But they knew from the onset that the lean years would come. They did not work with the insight that Joseph had. The state worked with only 20% of the production of the abundant years and was still able to sustain its entire population and the other nations that surrounded them. What happened to the 80% from the seven years of abundance? Could it be that they wasted it and abused it while banking on the state grant?

South Africa fought a bitter struggle against the evil system of Apartheid. Upon attainment of freedom in 1994, the country has steadily declined to a hollow shell of its apartheid era. Some people have even voiced a longing for the Apartheid days, "because there were jobs." In 2020, the state is handing out R14billion monthly to around 16 million grant recipients. That is nearly 25% of the population. After the COVID-19 crisis, another vast majority do not qualify for the state grant by a narrow margin will become eligible. With a recession and rising unemployment, this will simply be unsustainable.

But you need to know that South Africans are some of the most creative and brilliant Africans you can find on the continent. Their country is blessed with unimaginable natural resources from gold, diamond, platinum, land, seas and colourful cultural diversity. So, what is wrong? I am convinced that the problem is the 80:20 crisis. In truth, 80% potential of South African opportunity remains untapped while the rest of the nation relies on the 20% capacity of the state. There is a terrible cycle of trading votes for food. It is not surprising that a quarter of a century after apartheid elections are still won on the promises to "look after the poorest of the poor."

Like most African states, the generation that fought the struggle against colonialism and oppression did far more than their free fellow citizens. There are exceptions of course, but in the main, that is the tragedy of the continent. The best years in leadership, cultural expression, politics, arts and science are predominantly in the past. But, the political leaders of the struggle saw this with recently liberated African states. One wonders where they got it wrong to take the same route.

Had the Egyptians heeded Joseph's advice, they would have contributed 20%, saved 30% and spent 50% and they would have had surplus for export and earned revenue from the savings in their individual capacities - without need to resort to the state for sustenance. An American president once remarked that the measure of a successful State Welfare program is the number of people who are leaving it rather than those who join!

Biblical economics both in the Old and New Testaments advocates for private ownership of the means of production (i.e. land), diligent productive work, and generosity. Whether it is the Land Laws which prohibited the selling of land and its unconditional return after 50 years if it had been leased under desperate circumstances, the parables of Jesus about farming and investment or the church members contributing to common fund from personal resources. The basic premise for this is that everyone has capacity for creativity and productivity, allowing them to convert primary resources into products and goods that can be sold leading to increased personal wealth that aggregates into national wealth.

27

No African Dream

The most attractive thing about America is the concept of the 'American Dream.' The notion that there is an opportunity created by the state and the laws of the land for any private enterprise to thrive through hard work. It is common knowledge that this is not always the case, but that a nation holds that as a central tenet, is a feat of enviable proportions. It keeps people willing to work harder or to try again! A vision is not for a state, but for the people!

The Soviet socialist policies failed not because they were bad in themselves. On paper they were really good, but in practice centralised economies soon fell prey to human flaws of selfishness, greed and double standards. The value of sharing is best encouraged from a position of personal abundance and wealth. The years of abundance would precede the lean years so the people would learn generosity from abundance.

Paul reiterates this through his admonishing of the redeemed believers; *"He who has been stealing must steal no longer, but must work, doing something useful with his own hands, that he may have something to share with those in need." (Eph 4:28) NIV.* Note that he moves from lack (leading to stealing) to abundance (sharing) with those in need. Effective generosity is impossible from poverty and lack!

Voluntary Slavery

The Egyptians' neglect of this personal responsibility and dependence on the state cost them not only their wealth, but their freedom as well. The desperation was so great that they were willing to give up their freedom for survival. Gen 47:18-24 records:

When that year was over, they came to him the following year and said, "We cannot hide from our lord the fact that since our money is gone and our livestock belongs to you, there is nothing left for our lord except our bodies and our land. 19 Why should we perish before your eyes — we and our land as well? Buy us and our land in exchange for food, and we with our land will be in bondage to Pharaoh. Give us seed so that we may live and not die, and that the land may not become desolate." NIV

They offered themselves in bondage to Pharaoh when their money and livestock ran out and there were still years of famine left. The lean years were as severe as they were predicted to be. It was not Joseph's fault or Pharaoh's. They were not exploited but they failed to plan - using a principle that worked well for the state but not for them, despite the fact that the state only had a quarter of the resources they had and no capacity to multiply it. The state built the reserves out of savings only. They had the option of savings as well as trade.

20 So Joseph bought all the land in Egypt for Pharaoh. The Egyptians, one and all, sold their fields, because the famine was too severe for them. The land became Pharaoh's, 21 and Joseph reduced the people to servitude, from one end of Egypt to the other. 22 However, he did not buy the land of the priests, because they received a regular allotment from Pharaoh and had food enough from the allotment Pharaoh gave them. That is why they did not sell their land. NIV

After this transaction, the whole land belonged to Pharaoh. There was one exception though, the land of the priests. They did not sell it because they had a contingency plan. The Egyptians certainly would have saved their lands if they had taken heed to the formula that Joseph gave at the beginning. If Egypt had nothing left, then Joseph's formula would have been a farce. But it was not. Egypt had food, while they were selling off their livelihood and assets and handing themselves over to be enslaved.

> 23 Joseph said to the people, "Now that I have bought you and your land today for Pharaoh, here is seed for you so you can plant the ground. 24 But when the crop comes in, give a fifth of it to Pharaoh. The other four-fifths you may keep as seed for the fields and as food for yourselves and your households and your children." NIV

The sad thing about this is that even though the Egyptians had voluntarily given themselves over to Pharaoh, they were now in a set routine. They extended the servitude and accepted the new arrangement even after it ceased to be necessary. They did not protest or negotiate their freedom. It is sad that we get used to the circumstances that befall us so long as we can get by. But God's plan is not for us to get by, but to thrive. No one can thrive in bondage.

The system of bondage started with a desperate circumstance and did not have to continue forever, but the Egyptians did not challenge the situation. We have seen some previously poor nations emerge to become debt-free and stable middle-income countries. It is true that this takes more than policy shifts in government. It takes individuals working hard for the future of their nation and giving up instant success and seeking the long-term welfare of their nations. Government policy aids the process but cannot make it happen. It is surprising that some of the poorest countries have the richest people on the continent with resources stashed away in foreign accounts often wasted in frivolous lifestyles. That is the tragedy of material success and a poverty mentality. Someone poignantly said such are *"so poor, all they have is money!"*

The spirit of entrepreneurship

Entrepreneurship is what causes certain individuals to thrive while others wallow in self-pity. It makes them millionaires without looting state resources or exploiting the poor. Joseph's prediction and his proposal was supposed to spawn multitudes of entrepreneurs because he outlined the blueprint for a new culture. Unfortunately, the Egyptians were content following him on the local press and 'social media!' They must have venerated him as a maverick Jewish whiz kid or a guy with powerful government connections. After all he could interpret dreams or maybe Potiphar set him up. In every generation, stories abound about successful entrepreneurs, but few can replicate their success. Joseph's blueprint reflects a culture that we fail to adopt in our own private lives, yet it works for others and we have them as living proof.

Identify opportunity

Joseph understood from the interpretation of the dreams that there were going to be seven years of plenty followed an equal number by famine. He set out to maximise those years that brought abundance. He understood that the opportunity window was not forever and made hay while the sun shone.

Work with targets

Once he saw the opportunity he worked with targets, He calculated how much grain he would collect and where to store it. He paced himself well with 20% every year for seven years. He did not overwhelm himself as most of us do trying to get rich quickly. Biting more than we can chew!

Mobilise resources

Joseph did not work alone. He had the natural and human resources of Egypt at his disposal and did not waste any. He made them work for him. From the onset, he let Pharaoh know that this operation would not be a one-man show. The person appointed to the task would need to work with a team of commissioners.

Plan for the long term

Joseph understood that although he was saving food in the short term, it was for the long-term sustenance of the nations. "To save lives as you see today!" (50v20) His vision was beyond personal wealth and dealing with the impending crisis.

This long-term projection is what has helped many successful nations and organisations. Their aim is not to produce some iconic individuals but to make maximum impact in the world. The change of administration and absence of a long-term vision has been the undoing of many nations.

Understand the operating environment

The first thing we are told about Joseph after his appointment is that he 'travelled throughout Egypt.' He had a limited scope despite his wisdom. He had spent most of his time in a local space. We can be sure that he met people, identified sites and gained a clearer picture of the country's size and the kind of administration that would be needed to manage the logistics of the collection and distribution of the food. Entrepreneurship is never by luck or random strikes. It thrives on research and appropriate information. As we have come to know, travel and actual contact with people on the ground plays a great deal in creating extensive entrepreneurial programs and leading well.

The underpinnings of entrepreneurship

Every civilisation and every nation started with a bunch of people and raw materials and they built it from scratch. Every thriving enterprise or influential organisation also started this way: One or a few people with ideas, sheer hard work and they made history. King Solomon who ruled after his father David, was born with the proverbial silver spoon in his mouth. He was born in the time when David his father had worked had to consolidate the kingdom of Israel and during a time of peace. His ascent to the throne was secured by his father's loyal lieutenants against rival siblings.

However, Solomon built a great reputation as an entrepreneur as he was endowed with unprecedented wisdom and grace from God. In his books of Wisdom, he reflects on the meaning of life, wealth, hard work and success. He also shares his personal experiences of both wisdom and folly. The book of

Ecclesiastes, which is regarded as his memoirs, tells of how he came to be the wealthiest man in his time:

4 I undertook great projects: I built houses for myself and planted vineyards. 5 I made gardens and parks and planted all kinds of fruit trees in them. 6 I made reservoirs to water groves of flourishing trees. 7 I bought male and female slaves and had other slaves who were born in my house. I also owned more herds and flocks than anyone in Jerusalem before me. 8 I amassed silver and gold for myself, and the treasure of kings and provinces. I acquired men and women singers, and a harem as well — the delights of the heart of man. 9 I became greater by far than anyone in Jerusalem before me. In all this my wisdom stayed with me. - (Eccl 2:4-9) NIV

He lists no less than 14 lucrative projects that he initiated in a range of fields and industries. This is the man who made silver as common as stone in Jerusalem and had a fleet of ships that brought incredible wealth. (1 Kings 9-10). He propounds entrepreneurship's risk-taking, when he says:

Cast your bread upon the waters, for after many days you will find it again. 2 Give portions to seven, yes to eight, for you do not know what disaster may come upon the land. 3 If clouds are full of water, they pour rain upon the earth. Whether a tree falls to the south or to the north, in the place where it falls, there will it lie. 4 Whoever watches the wind will not plant; whoever looks at the clouds will not reap. As you do not know the path of the wind, or how the body is formed in a mother's womb, so you cannot understand the work of God, the Maker of all things. 6 Sow your seed in the morning, and at evening let not your hands be idle, for you do not know

which will succeed, whether this or that, or whether both will
do equally well. (Eccl 11:1-6) NIV

Solomon was incredibly wealthy and yet immensely generous! He understood that the wealth acquired did not define the owner and his philosophy was that life was too short to be focused on accumulating things without a relationship with God and fellow mankind. This principle he teaches with many of his proverbs and wise sayings. Jesus had a very unconventional attitude towards money and success. Yet he had both at his disposal. He taught the same in the parable of the rich fool in Luke 12:15-21:

Then he said to them, "Watch out! Be on your guard against all kinds of greed; a man's life does not consist in the abundance of his possessions." 16 And he told them this parable: "The ground of a certain rich man produced a good crop. 17 He thought to himself, 'What shall I do? I have no place to store my crops.' 18 "Then he said, 'This is what I'll do. I will tear down my barns and build bigger ones, and there I will store all my grain and my goods. 19 And I'll say to myself, "You have plenty of good things laid up for many years. Take life easy; eat, drink and be merry." ' 20 "But God said to him, 'You fool! This very night your life will be demanded from you. Then who will get what you have prepared for yourself?' 21 "This is how it will be with anyone who stores up things for himself but is not rich toward God."-NIV

He reiterates this in his parable about a shrewd manager who was faced with the imminent loss of employment and income and changed his attitude towards money from hoarding it to sharing it with the future in mind:

2 Jesus told his disciples: "There was a rich man whose manager was accused of wasting his possessions. 2 So he called him in and asked him, 'What is this I hear about you? Give an account of your management, because you cannot be manager any longer.' 3 "The manager said to himself, 'What shall I do now? My master is taking away my job. I'm not strong enough to dig, and I'm ashamed to beg— 4 I know what I'll do so that, when I lose my job here, people will welcome me into their houses.' 5 "So he called in each one of his master's debtors. He asked the first, 'How much do you owe my master?' 6 "'Eight hundred gallons of olive oil,' he replied. "The manager told him, 'Take your bill, sit down quickly, and make it four hundred.' 7 "Then he asked the second, 'And how much do you owe?' "'A thousand bushels of wheat,' he replied." He told him, 'Take your bill and make it eight hundred.' 8 "The master commended the dishonest manager because he had acted shrewdly. For the people of this world are more shrewd in dealing with their own kind than are the people of the light. 9 I tell you, use worldly wealth to gain friends for yourselves, so that when it is gone, you will be welcomed into eternal dwellings. NIV

At one point he also preconditioned the sale of everything and giving to the proceeds to the poor to one wannabe follower. The man went away sad because he was very wealthy.

23 Then Jesus said to his disciples, "I tell you the truth, it is hard for a rich man to enter the kingdom of heaven. 24 Again I tell you, it is easier for a camel to go through the eye of a needle than for a rich man to enter the kingdom of God."

- Matt 19:23-24NIV

Recovery is possible.

It is true that entrepreneurship (the wisdom to make money and utilize it for maximum good) will be the way towards recovery from the impact of COVID-19. Already we saw that the countries that managed to bounce back from the initial impact of the coronavirus are those that have experienced a similar situation before and learnt how to anticipate similar scenarios in the future. South Korea, China and Singapore are some of those that managed to contain the situation early on. They used lessons learnt from the past and acted in response to the potential disaster that befell those countries that were complacent. They employed three entrepreneurial leadership factors i.e. resolve, people and hard work.

Resolve

There was a clear resolve by the leadership on how to deal with the crisis. They were not waiting for guidelines from the World Health Organisation (WHO) or funding from donors. Interestingly, South Korea's Moon was also facing an election year like the USA's Trump, but his style of leadership did not gravitate towards politicking as was seen with Trump, who gave America a false sense of security even calling the virus "kung-fu virus." Egypt's survival under Joseph depended on Pharaoh and his council's decision and they were resolute. They acted decisively, immediately appointing Joseph and giving him the authority and resources to make the plan work. Every crisis calls for quick decisive leadership. Indecisive leadership will cause suffering that could be prevented.

The people

The cordial relationship between the people and the leadership was commendable in these countries. They did not need to resort to draconian lockdown procedures. Wuhan City is the same size as London and yet the citizens stayed indoors for the duration of the lockdown. Sadly, in some instances in smaller places in South Africa we saw complete disregard for the lockdown rules and even looting of liquor stores! People are irrational in time of crisis. Their fear becomes greater than reason and they act on survival impulses. It was on two occasions that Cyril Ramaphosa, the South African president was criticized for postponing a scheduled national address. Even though, there was a need for extensive consultation, it is important that the leader is visible and engages with the people in crisis times. As one person said during those anxious moments; "What we need now is leadership and not a plan!"

It is also important that people are managed to co-operate with the leadership during a crisis. Some nations just unleashed the might of the state against the citizens, beating them up, arresting them and enforcing lockdown measures without contingency plans. This is cruel leadership and it often exacerbates rather than alleviate a crisis. Empathetic leaders do not use themselves as a standard but the most vulnerable to make laws in a crisis.

Hard work

The build-up of the reserves and ensuring that they are adequate for the stretch of seven years takes meticulous planning. Joseph had to put an accountability system in place to manage local distribution as well as the exports. The Egyptians on the other hand, lacked a system of managing surplus. They revelled in the abundance of the moment and did not think about developing capacity to carry more. This is the challenge many of our nations. We are taken by surprise because we are near sighted or we never seriously pursue our plans. Building capacity is hard but it must be done.

Looking to the future

Hope is an asset in the times of devastation. Those countries that recovered quickly in the initial stages of the COVID-19 pandemic are those that did not resign themselves to fate. They managed the spread of despondency in the wake of all sorts of apocalyptic speculation and conspiracy theories with tens of thousands dying daily and being buried in mass graves. They worked hard to keep hope alive despite their limited understanding of the virus. That hope was alive, mattered more than their limited scientific capabilities. This is to be contrasted with those who falsified the figures and kept their citizens in the dark. Hope thrives against the odds not without!

What was certain in Egypt from the onset of the 14-year period was that after the seven years of abundance there would be seven lean years. That those lean years would be so severe that the good years would be forgotten. Then after that very difficult period, normalcy would return. The poor Egyptians made far reaching trade-offs that went beyond the predetermined period of suffering. They lost hope. There is not much that you can do for a hopeless person. They failed to capitalise on the surplus of the good years but also emerged losers after the severe years of famine.

In uncertain times every nation or organisation needs leaders who are hopeful. It needs people who are resilient. People who look for opportunities in crisis. People who know that survival is possible. Those who understand that when you hit rock-bottom there is only one way to go: That would be - up!

Chapter 3

Step up to Lead

Joseph is known as 'the dreamer.' Like many leaders, he is idolised as only his extraordinary gifts are highlighted. I am grateful to Guy Brandon's article that helped me realise that even though Joseph was a great leader the long-term impact of this splendid plan included some undesirable side effects!

Crisis is always an opportunity for leadership. It could be crisis at global, national, organizational or even at family level. Leaders step up to lead. One ought not shy away from leadership because of personal limitations. In fact, some of the finest leaders in history had major faults, setbacks and limitations. They led well despite those handicaps. As pointed out earlier, every leader functions under the unction of the Spirit of God. That, however, does not exonerate the leader from personal responsibility for their failings and seeking to improve their capacity to be a better leader.

Dealing with pain

Joseph's life story is that of struggle and pain. He struggled with painful experiences for most of his life. His brothers sold him into slavery at age seventeen. Those memories must have challenged his personal sense of worth and maybe drove him to be the high achiever he was – to prove that he was worth something. However, his dysfunctional family was not his only challenge, he suffered a setback when he was falsely accused and imprisoned for his upright stance against his Madam's advances.

When he finally stands before Pharaoh, he had been forgotten for two years by a 'beneficiary' of his gift! After his appointment as Prime Minister in Egypt, he got married and the naming of his Children hints at his struggle with pain in Gen 41:50-52

50 Before the years of famine came, two sons were born to Joseph by Asenath daughter of Potiphera, priest of On. 51 Joseph named his firstborn Manasseh and said, "It is because God has made me forget all my trouble and all my father's household." 52 The second son he named Ephraim and said, "It is because God has made me fruitful in the land of my suffering."

The firstborn is named to forget all the troubles of his father's household and the second speaks about comfort in the land of his suffering. Both sons immortalize the pain he endured. During the second phase of the famine, a second layer of pain was yet to be uncovered when his brothers came to Egypt to buy grain:

8 Although Joseph recognized his brothers, they did not recognize him. 9 Then he remembered his dreams about

them and said to them, "You are spies! You have come to
see where our land is unprotected." (Gen 42:8-9)

Although this accusation was a cover-up, it reveals the struggle that he had in dealing with his brothers. Here he was in Egypt with a son whose name celebrated his forgetting the hardships and his father's household and yet today these same brothers that ignored his pleas for mercy are standing before him reminding him of all the things he thought were in the past. It took two trips back and forth between Egypt and Canaan for him to figure out a way around this pain.

Leaders must deal with their personal pain to be able to empathise with the pain of others. Forgetting it may not even be desirable, but healing is certainly required if one will lead well. It is likely that Joseph's policies of servitude for the Egyptians may have been inspired by some level of insecurity as a leader in his own life. He doesn't get to forgive his brothers until the second year of the famine years and these policies are already in operation. Maybe they were designed to secure the throne of the Pharaoh against some unforeseen betrayal.

Of course, this is mere speculation, but many leaders take a hard stance because they have had painful experiences and learnt the hard way about human failings. They have been hurt, betrayed and stabbed in the back. Very few of us take the reins without wounds. Hopefully, our wounds turn into scars – reminding us of our hurts without pain! The use of power with pain is a dangerous combination. Many cruel leaders have taught us and left indelible marks on the sands of history. The healing of the leader's hurts is important because they wield several dimensions of power that can quickly get off the rails if unchecked. Hurt hibernates and erupts in violent forms when power changes hands. Hurt people hurt others. So, a leader must heal to lead well.

Gift Power

Joseph has power on several levels when he takes leadership. He has the supernatural gift of interpreting dreams. That is what makes him stand before kings and not obscure men!

> *A man's gift makes room for him,*
> *and brings him before great men.*
> *(Prov 18:16) NKJV*

Although there is evidence that suggests that in his youth, he may have mishandled his gift and got himself in trouble with his brothers in the first place. He is mature now and does not abuse that power over Pharaoh. Scriptural evidence shows us that Joseph enjoyed a great deal of respect from Pharaoh all through his career as a leader.

A leader who leads through their gift makes profound impact on those the lead. It is sad that many assume leadership by winning a popular vote rather than by their gifting distinguishing them as a fit for the task at hand. Indeed, gifting must be balanced by other factors such as resources, team etc. Otherwise it can become warped and manipulative, doing more harm than good. A gift is given to serve others and not the owner or it quickly turn exploitative. Nonetheless, it is a critical factor to bring to the task of leadership.

Official power

Joseph's ascent to power is sudden, but he has proved himself as a capable manager of people and resources. In Potiphar's house, his master left everything under his care. In prison, the warden left all the king's prisoners under his care. Pharaoh now appoints him over the nation and leaves everything under his care. It feels like a natural progression over thirteen years! He is publicly appointed to the office of Prime Minister in Egypt and he is second in command to Pharaoh and he is only junior to him regarding the throne!

That amount of power has caused untold suffering for people that some leaders exercise over them. That is why the Bible discourages the appointment of novices to senior positions. This power must be exercised in conjunction with others. The relational dynamic is an important factor for checks and balances. The leaders must act in the best interest of those that they lead. Unfortunately, running for office in many contexts is synonymous to running for the power, prestige and benefits that come with it. It is unwise to give absolute power to any individual, no matter how good they are.

Everyone has their blindside. Despite all his experience, Joseph had his fair share of blunders in office. The post-crisis enslavement of the Egyptians, hoarding cash and making them buy the food they had contributed as well as acquiring their land for food hardly resemble just policies. Joseph seems to have resorted to run a slave-state in collusion with Pharaoh. His interests were taken care of and so were those of his family. That smells like contemporary politics, right?

Moral Power

Even though he had not majored in Economics and Social Science - Joseph was an upright man. For this, he became Pharaoh's greatest appointments. He knew his limits and controlled his desires. He had a fear of God that was unquestionable and was determined to go to lengths to maintain his loyalty to those who trusted him. Whether it was Potiphar with his wife, the jail warden with the prisoners or Pharaoh with the whole of Egypt. He is a model of personal integrity.

Many leaders get overwhelmed by the freebies that come with the position of power and fall from grace with scandals of abuse of office. This is the power that every leader must develop on their own and by the company they keep. After all, the Bible warns that bad company corrupts good morals. A leader with a shady private life is often a puppet of those that know their secrets. This often becomes the leak in the boat that eventually causes it to sink.

Spiritual power

The distinguishing factor that can be seen throughout Joseph's life is the hand of God and his blessing upon the man. Leadership comes with spiritual authority. Unfortunately, many leaders seek to maintain their dominance over their followers through dark spiritual power. The leader's spirituality is no small thing. It is highly contested turf because whatever controls the leader controls the people. We live in a world that pretends that leaders can lead without spiritual influence. Nothing could be further from the truth. All leadership from the throne to the household is accountable to God and by default it is spiritual. The spirituality of leadership determines the state of the nation or family.

The scripture by making a direct link between leadership and national welfare urges us to take spiritual responsibility for those in leadership in 1 Tim 2:1-5:

1 I urge, then, first of all, that requests, prayers, intercession and thanksgiving be made for everyone— 2 for kings and all those in authority, that we may live peaceful and quiet lives in all godliness and holiness. 3 This is good, and pleases God our Savior, 4 who wants all men to be saved and to come to a knowledge of the truth.

Power of Choice

Probably the greatest demonstration of power for Joseph in his leadership and personal life was the decision to forgive people. We should not assume for a moment that this was easy "because he was such a spiritual man!" Yet he had to do it. He had to forgive the guy who forgot him. He had to forgive Potiphar who jailed him unfairly and his wife who false accused him of attempted rape. He had to choose not to use his newly acquired position above them to be vindictive. He had to let go of the things that hurt him most. His naming his children sounds like a deliberate step in that direction.

However, the ultimate test came when he came face to face with his conniving, plotting and hateful brothers. Most people can bear the scorn of the enemy and stranger, but not their own family. Joseph had to face this and forgive. The process was long. It started with the sight of his brothers triggering memories of nearly two decades before. They reminded him of his pleas for mercy that they ignored. How they scorned him and taunted his as 'the dreamer.' They put him in a well, stripped him of his coat of many colours, the best thing he ever possessed! He was chained and lost his youthful years away from his dad and little brother. What kind of brothers do such things to their own?

Now the Dream was fulfilled right before their eyes. He was right after all. God is vindicating him now! He was having his last laugh. But God wanted him to know that vengeance is His. That his brothers had a plan, but God thwarted it and His plan was in action all along. He was showing him that He would be rejected himself and refused by his own people and yet he would love them still. Ultimately, that they would choose a murderer in His place and reject and crucify Him and that he would still forgive them for they do not know what they do!

Forgiveness is the greatest power because it is given to an undeserving person, by the victim and without condition. It is the ultimate power. Once it is preconditioned, it loses its power. Yet it is only possible because we realise that there is a greater process beyond our unfortunate circumstances.

Step up to lead
The responsibility to lead does not wait for us to recover. It does not exempt us from the struggles of life. We are called upon to seek healing while we lead. To examine our lives to

see if our leadership is influenced by negative experiences and expectations, a selfish drive or disregard for others.

But there are leaders who have perpetuated the hurts and pains of the past. They took the opportunity to avenge age-old vendettas or marginalise other people. They feel justified to do so because of what happened to them in history. There is little hope for progress and thriving or even survival for such leaders and those they lead.

A time of crisis can help us unearth some of the deep-seated things that we thought we had dealt with. It can be a great opportunity to empathise. To demonstrate integrity and raise around us people who share a servant heart. Throughout the COVID-19 outbreak, the leaders who shone were those that served their people, empathized and comforted and took great risks for the people. They are the leaders who give hope.

Chapter 4

Lessons for leaders

Joseph's leadership is a powerful illustration of the possibility of leadership. He is a leader who steps up to lead. Your leadership journey emerges out of your life experiences. There is no useless experience. In fact, his father had identified that capacity in him early in life and unfortunately did not mentor him well. But the fact that we are not well mentored does not mean we are not called to lead!

Mentorship

Mentorship starts with the identifying of leadership potential, usually at an early age or on the fringes. It is a wise leader who employs mentorship to perpetuate their legacy and ideals through others. Sadly, many leaders are the centrepiece of their leadership story and stay in front forever! When their term ends, so does their leadership. Mentorship is not only about succession, but also the multiplying the good of leadership. It is enabling others to rise and live up to their potential for leadership. A mentor is an enabler. A multiplier.

Joseph's father identified this in him. He must have seen signs of this potential and made sure the boy was close to him. He himself had been in a bad succession feud that nearly cost him his life. He had sons from his concubines and the other wife, Leah, but Rachel was his choice and his firstborn son with her was to be his successor in the Abrahamic covenant succession. He made Joseph an elaborate gown and gave him responsibility over his brothers. So, when the dreams came, he must have felt they were a confirmation of his plan.

Potential is all a mentee needs to qualify for mentorship. Their skills will be refined through responsibilities given and maturity over time. But God had a greater plan for Joseph so he needed a more efficient mentorship schedule for him than his father could provide. So, he sent him to Egypt.

> 17 and he sent a man before them — Joseph, sold as a slave. 18 They bruised his feet with shackles, his neck was put in irons, 19 till what he foretold came to pass, till the word of the Lord proved him true. 20 The king sent and released him, the ruler of peoples set him free. 21 He made him master of his household, ruler over all he possessed, 22 to instruct his princes as he pleased and teach his elders wisdom. (Ps 105:17-22) NIV

Responsibility

There is no leadership without responsibility. There is no greater frustration than being assigned a position and then deprived the capacity to act. It is better to be without the title but have responsibility. Joseph is taken to Egypt as a slave, but soon gets assigned his first responsibility in the house of a senior government official. This is no coincidence. God was guiding him. Here he soon is left in charge of everything except his master's food. What that implies is that he became as good at handling that household as Potiphar himself was!

Capacity grows with responsibility. While he was at home, he oversaw just 10 shepherd brothers who hated him and with whom he interacted occasionally. Now he oversaw an entire household of a senior government official and obviously rubbed shoulders with other very significant people. To do this, Potiphar must have become his mentor. He used to stay close to his dad who probably smothered him with his overprotective favouritism. Now he was being groomed to represent his influential master at national level. He became Potiphar's attendant or personal assistant!

Maturity
Joseph seems to have fallen into his bothers' bad books because he seemed to have had a knack for nosiness. He was an immature spoiled brat in their eyes, whatever the bad report that he brought to their father was about them. Now in Potiphar's house, he had to be mature in handling others, especially if that resulted in serious conflict as it did with his master's wife. He does not report her to her husband, nor does he quit his job. There is great maturity in the way he handles those he disagrees with him at this stage.

Leaders who are mature do not carry grudges or spend time trying to pull down their opponent or even trying to justify themselves from the tarnishing smear campaigns of their opponents. One such leader was Nehemiah, who when his opponents tried to discourage him with false reports and hiring internal moles responded by saying:

"I am carrying on a great project and cannot go down. Why should the work stop while I leave it and go down to you?" 4 Four times they sent me the same message, and each time I gave them the same answer. (Neh 6:3-4) NIV

Jesus is another who had a sell-out on his team who was not genuine from the start, he never spent his time distracted by Judas Iscariot. He let the wheat grow with the tares until the end where they were easily separated.

Authority

Leadership comes with authority. In times of crisis you are expected to use that authority. It is interesting that those who do not use the authority they are given are often judged harsher than those who do even if the results are not good – or even disastrous sometimes! When Joseph is assigned authority, he is clear where that starts and where it ends. Authority is the capacity to exercise leadership. Joseph is appointed to act for the good of those that he serves.

The lines are clearly drawn, he is second in command. He has power over all of Egypt and its people. He is tasked with executing the national plan as detailed in the proposal that he made to Pharaoh and was approved by his officials. He is to work with the commissioners assigned to the task. The extent of the leadership is measured against the authority that the leaders has. It is possible to overstep one's authority as much as it is to underutilize it. In both instances one's leadership is judged negatively. The use of authority is not to exploit those we have authority over. Even when we can get away with it. Authority works in tandem with trust and self-control. By the time we employ the law, the trust has already been breached. So, as that Centurion once said to Jesus:

> For I myself am a man under authority, with soldiers under me. I tell this one, 'Go,' and he goes; and that one, 'Come,' and he comes. I say to my servant, 'Do this,' and he does it."
> (Matt 8:9) NIV

One who would exercise authority over others must themselves be subject to the authority above them. No one who is lawless has the right to exercise authority over others.

Resources

Leadership is not magic. Every leader produces results with resources. Yes, there is an expectation to be innovative and improvise. However, no leader can produce results without adequate resources. Pharaoh is aware that Joseph has the Spirit of God and the wisdom required for this task, but he put people, money, transport and other essentials to be able to execute on the task. It was for the good of Egypt after all and Egypt had to fund the project.

It is unfortunate that in some contexts, the resources allocated for the work of service, are diverted for personal gain by greed and irresponsible leaders. In other cases, the senior leaders hoard the resources and yet expect those serving under them to produce results without adequate resources. There is no cruelty that exceeds the heartless leader who embezzles resources meant for public or team benefit. Equally, there is no shameful act as to benefit unduly from that which is meant for relief in a crisis. Leaders in all sectors are not immune to this. The lure of the forbidden, the pressure of the vultures around them and willing victims who present themselves as bait are always going to be there to contend with, but they are never a good excuse for a leader to let down their guard.

Accountability

Authority is always exercised with accountability. Leadership without accountability is a death trap for the leader and those they lead. Joseph is careful in his pronouncement of the formation of the office of the Prime Minister that this individual will act "under the authority of Pharaoh." Pharaoh himself was accountable to his officials and the priests.

At times of crisis, there are provisions for the leader to act arbitrarily with little or no consultation. This is the 'privilege' that every leader must exercise with maximum restraint and with much humility. They must also be willing to face the criticism should the result turn out to be less than desirable. In the case of a clear lapse in judgement, the leader may even have to be willing to step down from their position.

People

There is no leadership without people. The quality of the leader is always reflected through the people they lead. Leadership is serving. Joseph's job is not for his own personal dreams and great career. He understood that God's intention was to save many people. God gives leaders as a gift to his people. They make the best he put in them to come out and in times of crisis he uses the leaders to save many lives.

> But Joseph said to them, "Do not be afraid. Am I in the place of God? 20 You intended to harm me, but God intended it for good to accomplish what is now being done, the saving of many lives. 21 So then, do not be afraid. I will provide for you and your children." And he reassured them and spoke kindly to them. (Gen 50:19-21) NIV

Without leaders in times of crisis, the world would be an unbearable place to live in. Without leaders in the best times, the future would not be secured. Without leaders in the frontline, there would be no hope for the future.

Endnote

Lessons for leaders

The COVID-19 crisis has spotlighted leadership in very critical ways. For some an endorsement and for others an indictment. Here are a few key takeaways for leaders at every level.

Balance situational and strategic

Every crisis has those two dimensions. Situational leadership demands that you act immediately with what you have and manage the crisis in the best possible way. You must act with basic information and trust your gut feeling and consult a few trusted coleaders. Pharaoh did not start with setting up a commission to research this God etc. He and his court acted immediately. Strategic leadership focuses on the long term, asks sustainability questions and looks at the methodologies being employed to attain a result. Joseph looked at the entire 14-year period and beyond. Effective leadership strikes a good balance between these two perspectives.

Exposed vulnerability

Every crisis has significant losses, no matter how capable the leadership or how prepared you are. However, a lapse in the leadership's judgement can exacerbate the situation. We saw this in the complacent response of some leaders to the

COVID-19 crisis and the price they paid for it. Wise leaders learn from the experiences of others to avoid suffering the consequences themselves. Leaders are a covering for their people. Be wise.

Informed Decision
In a crisis, accurate information is your greatest arsenal. People tend to panic and untested information can have disastrous consequences. Wise leaders invest in quality information resources to make decisions during a crisis. Although in certain instances there is limited information, endeavour to create trust by being transparent and creating open collaboration between the leadership and the masses.

Lead beyond your constituency
Because our world is so interconnected, we recently discovered that our leadership decisions have a far greater reach than the physical jurisdiction of our leadership. So, Joseph discovered that his mandate was to save many lives when the Canaanites and people from other lands showed up at his doorstep to buy food. Lead without borders. Do not undermine your own capacity and ability to contribute to the quest for a solution to widespread crisis. Do not self-exclude. If you are excluded, include yourself!

Humble leadership
The people we lead want to survive and are willing to make reasonable trade-offs in a crisis. Left to themselves, people do not necessarily manage themselves with the vision and clarity. Leadership must guide people during times of crisis and not

exploit their dependence. To help them out of the crisis, to spare their lives. Leaders are a gift to the people they lead. Even though God had made him "like a father unto Pharaoh", he still understood that he was there to serve.

Leading where you are

Joseph became a great leader. He did not become an instant hit when Pharaoh invited him to join his court. He was noted for his leadership at Potiphar's house and in the jail house. He just got better and better. COVID-19 produced unlikely heroes in the form of health workers, previously unnoticed health ministers, as well as army and police officers. These people demonstrated their leadership by showing courage, caring for the dying, burying the deceased.

The call centres for trauma counselling, the pastors and the many essential service delivery personnel. The NGOs and regular neighbours organising large scale as well as local relief efforts are to be saluted. The value of frontline and visible leaders is to reproduce more leaders in every context during a crisis. It eases the burden on the leaders and utilises capacity that others have.

An effective leadership is that which helps those they lead to take responsibility for themselves and others during a crisis and not those that do everything for the people.

An ode to Leaders

Pray for your leaders. They are human.
Obey your leaders. They represent God.
Support your leaders, but do not idolize them.
Hold them accountable, but do not criticize them.
Care for leaders, but do not let them exploit you.
Forgive them when they fail and repent.
And when the lot falls on you to lead,
Step up and lead without fear.

www.ingramcontent.com/pod-product-compliance
Lightning Source LLC
Chambersburg PA
CBHW020619220526
45463CB00006B/2623